How to Deal with Anger

Metropolitan Youssef

How to Deal with Anger

By Metropolitan Youssef

Translation by St. Mary & St. Moses Abbey.

Designed & Published by:
St. Mary & St. Moses Abbey Press
101 S Vista Dr, Sandia, TX 78383
stmabbeypress.com

CONTENTS

Foreword

His Eminence Metropolitan Youssef charged me, in extreme humility, with the task of writing a foreword for his new books about family counseling. In truth, these books were riveting lectures His Eminence delivered to the students of Counseling Centers in several churches. They were then set in writing [for publication] as booklets, so that they may be used as references for the social and family lives of the children of the Church.

His Eminence Metropolitan Youssef, the Metropolitan of the Coptic Orthodox Diocese of the Southern United States, studied the science of counseling, with the permission and blessing of His Holiness Pope Shenouda III, until he completed a doctorate degree from the University of San Antonio after many years of studying. When the Church desired to benefit from this knowledge—to resolve many of the marital problems, to learn of the upright Christian ways of raising children, and [to benefit] the various fields of specialized services, such as the service of the elderly and the people with disabilities—His Eminence did not hold back from devoting the time of his rest, which he spent in Egypt, to teach these courses, whether in dioceses, or in numerous churches and also in the Institute of Pastoral Care in Cairo. He offered the labor and weariness of long travel and a great effort in the lectures that went on for hours, besides the small meetings which were held for the growth of the Counseling Centers and for the development of the curricula for teaching.

Our Church, under the leadership of the discerning, enlightened mind of His Holiness, our blessed Father, Pope Shenouda III, is indebted to His Eminence Metropolitan Youssef who is the pioneer of this service.

Knowing His Eminence for many years, we being fellow workers in the service in St. Anthony Church, Shobra, I write an introduction for a humble, self-denying personality, because His Eminence is neither drawn to praise, nor does he hate criticism, nor pursues fame; these virtues adorn the spiritual man and the faithful servant who gives honor to Whom honor is due, Who gives and blesses the gifts and talents.

May the Lord give His Eminence health and vigor, and may He take away from him the wars of Satan; and may He give each person hearing the word of God out of his blessed mouth, enlightenment, knowledge, and correction of the pedagogical errors.

His Grace Bishop Daniel
General Bishop of Ma'adi and Basateen

INTRODUCTION

Is anger a sin or not?

This question is often asked by many. The Holy Scriptures actually speak about the anger of God in numerous places. We also pray, saying, "Take away Your anger from us."[1] So, had anger been a sin, we, of course, could not have ascribed it to God. Often we hear of "godly anger," so how is it that anger is a sin and at the same time, we characterize it as godliness? Moreover, the Holy Scripture mentions, "Be angry, and do not sin: do not let the sun go down on your wrath."[2] How can we then interpret the word "be angry?"

Anger, in itself, is an energy. Every energy we can use constructively, and likewise, we can also use it destructively. We need energy that we may erect a building, and we also need it to demolish another building. We could use this energy in construction if it were steered in a sound direction. Likewise, we could use it in destruction if it were steered in the wrong direction.

1 Morning Raising of Incense.

2 Ephesians 4:26.

Therefore, when we speak of anger, we say, "How can we manage anger," and not, "How can we eradicate anger?" How do I steer the energy of anger for construction, and not for destruction, that I may benefit from it in building and growing my relationships with others, and also in edifying myself?

Moreover, the energy of anger may lead to other sins if it were not controlled, which is likened to a car driving down a road. The car is energy; if the driver controls it and subjugates it, it then accomplishes many good things. However, if he were to lose control over it, then it would lead to disaster. Therefore, the Holy Scripture speaks to us about the anger which is not under the subjection of man, which then eventually leads him to falling into sin and committing numerous mistakes.

We will address, with explanation and analysis, several points related to the topic of anger.

1

Anger Leads to Sin

The Book of Genesis recounts:

> And in the process of time it came to pass that Cain brought an offering of the fruit of the ground to the LORD. Abel also brought of the firstborn of his flock and of their fat. And the LORD respected Abel and his offering, but He did not respect Cain and his offering. And Cain was very angry, and his countenance fell. So the LORD said to Cain, "Why are you angry? And why has your countenance fallen? If you do well, will you not be accepted? And if you do not do well, sin lies at the door. And its desire is for you, but you should rule over it."[3]

---

3 Genesis 4:3–7.

The story, briefly, is that both Cain and Abel offered a sacrifice to God. Abel offered a sacrifice of blood, which was according to God's will. We know that Adam and Eve—after they fell into sin and ate of the tree of which God had told them not to eat—found themselves naked, so God clothed them in tunics of skin.[4] And perhaps some may ask, "And from where did these tunics of skin come?" The tunics of skin imply that there were some animals that were slain. But why were these animals slain? The answer is because God wanted show them that "without shedding of blood there is no remission."[5] And Adam and Eve learned that when they desired to offer a sacrifice to God, it must be a sacrifice of blood. Undoubtedly, Adam and Eve passed on this matter to their children. Abel adhered to offering a sacrifice of blood, while Cain did not. Therefore, the Lord accepted Abel's sacrifice, while He did not accept Cain's, because Cain offered of the fruit of the ground as an offering to God.[6] As a result, Cain was angry and very upset. Let us examine together what happened.

The Lord said to Cain very important words. The Holy Scripture recounts: "But He did not respect Cain

4 See Genesis 3:21.

5 Hebrews 9:22.

6 See Genesis 4:3.

and his offering. And Cain was very angry, and his countenance fell. So the LORD said to Cain, 'Why are you angry? And why has your countenance fallen?'"[7]

This question is very important for the person who is feeling angry. What could Cain give as an answer to this question? I believe he would have answered, "I am angry, Lord, because you did not accept my sacrifice; and I am angry because You favor my brother Abel. You have accepted his sacrifice, but mine You did not accept. I am angry because You did not encourage me. Accept my sacrifice this time only and encourage me, and the next time, I will offer You a sacrifice of blood. You ask me, Lord, 'Why are you angry?' all the while You reject my sacrifice and You do not look to me. This matter has upset me exceedingly."

But Cain was angry because he wanted to break the commandment and, at the same time, not to be punished, and not have God be angry with him. If Cain were thinking this way, it would mean he was blaming God, because the cause of his anger is that God was in favor of his bother Abel, and that He did not encourage him. Therefore, God directed this question to him, "Why are you angry? And why has your countenance fallen?"[8] God

7 Genesis 4:5–6.

8 Genesis 4:6.

was looking for the true cause for his distress and anger, [insisting] that the true reason lies within him, and not without him.[9]

The true cause for his anguish is that he wanted to apply the commandment in his own way, and at the same time, he did not want anyone to tell him that this was wrong or right.

We could observe such a thing at the time of Communion. Someone might come late [to the Divine Liturgy]. He then tells the priest that he came late, and the priest tells him, "How about, my beloved, you do not take Communion today." He then gets angry and falls into [a state of] distress. Thus, he behaved exactly like Cain. He wants to break the law, but rather than taking responsibility for this anger, whereby saying to the priest, "I have sinned," he instead wants people to accept his breaking of the law. And he goes on to say, "This priest is strict and rigid, and by this he distances people from Church." He places the whole blame upon the priest, and refuses to take responsibility for his fault.

Therefore, after God said to Cain, "Why are you angry?"[10] He added, saying, "If you do well, will you not

9 i.e. inside of him and not outside of him.

10 Genesis 4:6.

be accepted?"[11] "If you do well," the true reason for your anger, Cain, lies in the fact that you have made a mistake and you do not want to bear the consequences of this mistake. And instead of being upset and blaming Me, the solution is that you correct this fault.[12] When you have corrected your fault, I will pardon you and accept you. But beware, Cain, that if you do not do well, there is a sin lying at the door.

As we have previously said, anger which a man is unable to subjugate, leads to sin. And it is as though God is saying to him, "Your anger will lead you to commit another sin, that is, murder." Indeed, he rose up against his bother and killed him.[13] "And if you do not do well, sin lies at the door. And its desire is for you, but you should rule over it."[14] That is, sin desires to make you fall into its net, but beware, for this will not give you an excuse, because you are able to rule over it. So do not come and say, "What do I do? I was forced[15] to commit this sin." It is true that sin has a desire for you, but you are able to rule over it.

---

11 Genesis 4:7.

12 Or: mistake.

13 See Genesis 4:8.

14 Genesis 4:7.

15 That is, unwillingly.

In the dialogue that went on between the Lord and Cain, God clarified to him the following points:

1. Anger Is Inside the Person

God said to him that the cause of this fault lies within you, and thereby you ought to bear the consequences of this fault. For if you put the blame on others as the cause of your anger, you will never be able to rid yourself of it.

Likewise, whenever I offer counseling to a person prone to wrath, he begins by aiming the blame at others. I, then, must teach him to bear the responsibility of his anger, and must help him realize that the cause of his anger lies in himself.

If a person comes to me and mentions that he gets angry because his manager at work is irritating, or because his wife is difficult to deal with, or because his children are trouble-makers, he implicates others as the cause of his anger. This person will never overcome anger. He puts the blame on others, and says, "For me to be able to overcome anger, others must change."

However, at the heart of the matter, he must bear the responsibility for his anger, and then he can do well. "If you do well, will you not be accepted?"[16]—That is, he must begin by correcting[17] and treating the causes of his anger, then he will be relieved. But if he does not do well, leaving the flames of anger growing fiercely within him against others, he will end up falling into sin. "Sin lies at the door. And its desire is for you, but you should rule over it."[18]

Saint Augustine divided anger into three degrees:

a. The inner anger, where agitation is within the heart, without it being expressed with manifest gestures. "Whoever is angry with his brother without a cause shall be in danger of the judgement."[19]
b. Anger that is associated with a word that expresses it, though it [i.e., the word] may not be have a wicked meaning except that it indicates the existence of anger. ("Whoever says to his brother, 'Raca!'"[20])

16 Genesis 4:7.
17 Or: reforming.
18 Genesis 4:7.
19 Matthew 5:22.
20 Ibid.

c. Anger that is associated with a manifest agitation with an evil word (rancor). ("Whoever says, 'You fool!'"[21])

2. Anger Leads to Strife

"An angry man stirs up strife, and a furious man abounds in transgression."[22] If there were people passing the time in conversation calmly, among whom cordiality reigned, and who were bound by friendship, then one of them got up, being agitated, and started speaking sharply with a loud voice, he would make them also raise their voices and they would get agitated; thereby strife would take place among them. The furious man abounds in transgressions, and from the intensity of his anger, he explodes like an inflated balloon, and then he falls into many transgressions.

The Holy Scripture says, "For as the churning of milk produces butter, and wringing the nose produces blood, so

21 Ibid.

22 Proverbs 29:22.

the forcing of wrath produces strife."[23] For anger leads to violence without, and bitterness within.[24]

Saint Dorotheos divides anger in a similar fashion:

a. Internal disturbance or agitation. He likens it to a charcoal that gives smoke right upon its ignition.
b. Anger. This refers to the internal disturbance accompanied by an external agitation. This takes place if we do not put out the piece of charcoal with internal calmness in the heart, [thereby] letting ill will and suspicion inflame it, until flames start.
c. Rancor. This occurs if anger persists for a long time. That is, we add to the piece of charcoal fuel or any flammable material, so anger is transformed into rancor. Then to put out the piece of charcoal, there is a need for toil and a great struggle.

Therefore, we should not permit anger, in any of its degrees, to have a place in our hearts, or on our lips, or in the movements of our members, nor even to merely pass

---

23 Proverbs 30:30.

24 i.e. Violence on the outside and bitterness on the inside.

through our thoughts, so that the speck is not converted into a plank, thereby its excision becomes difficult.

2

Kinds of Anger

There are two kinds of anger: godly anger and ungodly anger.

1. Godly Anger

One of the clear examples of godly anger can be found in the passage of the Holy Scriptures when Moses the Prophet came down from the mountain carrying the two tablets of the covenant. When he found the people worshiping the calf, "Moses' anger became hot, and he cast the tablets out of his hands and broke them at the foot of the mountain."[25]

Another example of godly anger is when the Master Christ went into the temple and overturned the tables

25 Exodus 32:19.

of the money changers and the seats of those who sold doves. "Then Jesus went into the temple of God and drove out all those who bought and sold in the temple, and overturned the tables of the money changers and the seats of those who sold doves. And He said to them, 'It is written, "My house shall be called a house of prayer," but you have made it a "den of thieves."'"[26] Moreover, it is known that the Master Christ did purify the temple twice; first, at the beginning of His service, mentioned in the second chapter of the Gospel of our teacher John, and the second time took place during Holy Week.[27]

There are many who try to justify their anger as being godly anger. However, so that we may judge ourselves and differentiate between godly anger and ungodly anger, we must ask ourselves the following three questions:

- What is the motive of my anger?
- What is the end[28] I want to reach from my anger?
- What is the means I am using to achieve this end?

26 Matthew 21:12–13.

27 See ibid.

28 Or: aim.

The only motive for godly anger is the love of God, and the zeal for the glory of God. Therefore, the Holy Scripture says about the disciples that when they saw the Master Christ driving out those who were buying and selling, "then His disciples remembered that it was written, 'Zeal for Your house has eaten Me up.'"[29]

Not every zeal is considered godly; there is also ungodly zeal. A good example for ungodly zeal is mentioned in the Holy Scripture: "But when the chief priests and scribes saw the wonderful things that He did, and the children crying out in the temple and saying, 'Hosanna to the Son of David!' they were indignant[30] and said to Him, 'Do You hear what these are saying?' And Jesus said to them, 'Yes. Have you never read, "Out of the mouth of babes and nursing infants You have perfected praise"?'"[31]

The difference between godly zeal and ungodly zeal in the two examples is that the motive in the first case is the love of God, but the motive in the second case is the love of self. The love of God must be the motive behind all our conducts, as our teacher Paul says, "For the love of Christ compels us."[32]

---

29 John 2:17.

30 The word in Arabic is a derivative of the word "anger."

31 Matthew 21:15–16.

32 2 Corinthians 5:14.

The chief priests and scribes tried to justify their anger as being godly anger, but in reality, the motive was jealousy from the Master Christ. They were jealous of Him when the multitudes cried out and said of Him that He was the King of Israel. They wanted the glory for themselves, and the motive behind their anger is the self.[33]

Moses the prophet, however, when he broke the tablets of the covenant, his motive was the love of God; how could the people abandon the God who brought them out of the land of Egypt with a strong hand and an outstretched arm,[34] and make a calf and say, "This is your god, O Israel, that brought you out of the land of Egypt!"[35] The motive behind zeal must be pure, and is only the love of God.

The aim of godly anger is construction,[36] and not destruction and demolition. Its aim is to lead the other to repentance. If you felt anger within you, and you felt that you want to take vengeance and destroy the other, then your anger could never be godly anger. Moses led the people to worship God and made them dash in

---

33 Or: ego.

34 See Psalm 136:12 (NKJV), and Second Canticle in Midnight Praises.

35 Exodus 32:4.

36 Or: correction, reformation.

pieces the calf;[37] his aim was reformation,[38] that the people change from worshiping the calf to worshiping God.

The aim of the Master Christ, also, when He drove out the sellers and buyers, was to purify the temple, and to emphasize that the temple is a place of prayer and not of merchandise.[39]

The aim of ungodly anger is always to destroy the other and to punish him; therefore, the means used is never without sin. How can I say that my anger is godly while I am fuming, insulting, and cursing? Godly means must be used to express godly anger.

We must examine ourselves, faithfully, "for what man knows the things of a man except the spirit of the man which is in him."[40] Ask yourself, "What is the motive behind my anger? Was it construction,[41] or destruction? And how did I express my anger? Was it in a wrong way or not?"

Ultimately, if the aim is pure, that is, construction, and the motive is the love of God, and the means is spotless and pure—then anger will be a godly anger.

---

37 See Exodus 32:20.

38 Or: correction.

39 See John 2:16.

40 1 Corinthians 2:11.

41 i.e. reformation.

Aside from this, anger is ungodly, and this is what we will explain next.

2. Ungodly Anger

Of the illustrative examples of ungodly anger is the following passage in the First Book of Samuel:

> Then David hid in the field. And when the New Moon had come, the king sat down to eat the feast. Now the king sat on his seat, as at other times, on a seat by the wall. And Jonathan arose, and Abner sat by Saul's side, but David's place was empty. Nevertheless Saul did not say anything that day, for he thought, "Something has happened to him; he is unclean, surely he is unclean." And it happened the next day, the second day of the month, that David's place was empty. And Saul said to Jonathan his son, "Why has the son of Jesse not come to eat, either yesterday or today?"
>
> So Jonathan answered Saul, "David earnestly asked permission of me to go to Bethlehem. And he said, 'Please let me go, for our family has a sacrifice in the city, and my brother has commanded me to be there. And now, if I have found favor in your eyes, please let me get away and see my brothers.' Therefore he has not come

> to the king's table."
>
> Then Saul's anger was aroused against Jonathan, and he said to him, "You son of a perverse, rebellious woman! Do I not know that you have chosen the son of Jesse to your own shame and to the shame of your mother's nakedness? For as long as the son of Jesse lives on the earth, you shall not be established, nor your kingdom. Now therefore, send and bring him to me, for he shall surely die."
>
> And Jonathan answered Saul his father, and said to him, "Why should he be killed? What has he done?" Then Saul cast a spear at him to kill him, by which Jonathan knew that it was determined by his father to kill David.
>
> So Jonathan arose from the table in fierce anger, and ate no food the second day of the month, for he was grieved for David, because his father had treated him shamefully.[42]

Saul's anger was an ungodly anger, because his motive was not the love of God but the love of himself. God had anointed David king, and Saul wanted to pass the kingship to his sons so that the kingdom may continue to bear his name, even after his death. His goal, therefore, was to destroy David and to kill him so that

42 1 Samuel 20:24–34.

he may not threaten his kingship. And the means with which he expressed his anger was characterized by losing his nerves on his son and by humiliating and insulting him. He also aimed a spear at him.

Wrath and bitterness are the traits of ungodly anger. In his epistle to the Ephesians, Paul the Apostle speaks of these two traits, saying, "Let all bitterness, wrath, anger, clamor, and evil speaking be put away from you."[43] So what is the difference between wrath and bitterness?

Remember that at the beginning of our discussion on this topic, we indicated that anger is an energy. So if the energy is directed outwardly, it is wrath; and if it is directed inwardly, it is bitterness.

Wrath is when a person loses his temper and becomes agitated, which may be transformed into violence and causing harm. When a person becomes angry, his voice is raised and he aims insults at others. He may hit, throw things to the ground, and break possessions, for wrath is explosion that can cause harm and damage to others, whether physically or psychologically.

As for bitterness, it is the suppressed [bottled-up] anger within. It is regrettable that some people, who consider themselves religious, think that when they

43 Ephesians 4:31.

suppress anger inside, this means they have overcome anger. They, however, are burning inwardly because their soul is bitter and thereby they feel bitterness.

Suppressed anger, if not expressed in a sound way, may lead to many illnesses such as stomach ulcer, high blood pressure, diabetes, and paralysis.

There is an example of wrath in the Gospel of our teacher St. Luke the Evangelist, when the Master Christ was speaking in the synagogue, but those listening were not impressed by His words, "so all those in the synagogue, when they heard these things, were filled with wrath."[44] But of what kind was this anger? It says in verse 29, "And [they] rose up and thrust him out of the city; and they led Him to the brow of the hill on which the city was built, that they might throw Him down over the cliff." Their anger here was transformed into violence, for they wanted to take the Master Christ to the brow of the hill that they might throw Him down [over the cliff]. This is the kind of anger we call "wrath" because it was transformed into violence.

We have discussed the definition of anger and we said that it is an energy, and that this energy has to be directed in a sound way so that it may be an energy

---

44 Luke 4:28.

used for building up[45] and not destruction. We also mentioned two kinds of anger: godly and ungodly anger. We categorized ungodly anger into two kinds: outward explosion (wrath), and inwardly suppressed anger (bitterness).

> "Your life with all its energy is a talent God has entrusted you with. Therefore you need to develop your personality, in general, that it may be transformed into a strong balanced personality, whether in the mind, or the conscience, or the will, or the knowledge, or the wisdom and the conduct, or the judgement of things, or the balanced temperament."

— His Holiness Pope Shenouda III —

45 i.e. edification.

3

Anger Management

Every person who tries to justify his anger by casting the blame on others will never be able to rid themselves of anger. I would like to draw your attention to a very important point, which is that anger is not a reaction to another's behavior, but rather a reaction to the interpretation of another's behavior.

What was the cause for Cain's anger? He interpreted God's rejection of his sacrifice in a particular manner. He thought that God was biased to Abel, and so He rejected his sacrifice. The cause of his anger is not God's position towards his sacrifice, but rather it is Cain's interpretation of the cause for which God rejected his sacrifice.

I present the following example to clarify this matter. If there is a group of people gathered together in one place, and someone walks in and directs a torrent of insults to all, will all have the same reaction, or will their reactions be different? Here we find that the action is one, but the reactions will be undoubtedly different. One might say, "Don't mind this person. He is crazy." Another might say, "How dare he insult us; it is not right that he did this!" Then [the latter one] may decide to go over and amicably speak with him, while another will not even think but will get up and hit him. There is yet another who will instantly return the insult.

What makes our behaviors different? It is because each of us has interpreted the other's behavior in a different way. Therefore, you have to bear the responsibility for your anger, because you yourself interpreted the other's behavior. I am not in possession[46] of the other's action, but I do possess my reaction. Here we arrive at the first point of how to manage anger.

Bear the responsibility for your anger

You have to bear full responsibility for your anger and confess it to yourself, and before God, and before your father of confession. Do not seek excuses for yourself. I would like to emphasize what we have previously said,

46 That is, I do not have power over the other's action.

that if you blame others for your anger, you will not gain victory over the sin of anger.

Let us reflect on what the Master Christ did when He went to the house of a person named Simon, and a sinful woman went in. What was Simon's reaction, and what was the reaction of the Master Christ? Simon became distressed and angry, and his anger led him to judging. So he said to himself, "This Man, if He were a prophet, would know who and what manner of woman this is who is touching Him, for she is a sinner."[47] Why did Simon become angry? Because he looked at this woman and interpreted her conduct as sinful, and then he became distressed.

The Master Christ, however, looked at this same woman, and while He did not deny that she was a sinner saying, "Your sins are forgiven,"[48] He furthermore saw that she loved much. This outlook made the Master Christ not become angry nor distressed.

Here is another example from Holy Scriptures, from the Gospel of our teacher St. John. They seized a woman who was caught in the very act, and were full of anger, and each was holding a stone in his hand. They said to the Lord Jesus, "Now Moses in the Law, commanded

47 Luke 7:39.

48 Luke 7:48.

us that such should be stoned."[49] But the Master Christ directed their attention to something else, so rather than looking *at* this woman, he made each of them look *into* himself. He said to them that the Law indeed says that such a woman should be stoned, but "he who is without sin among you, let him throw a stone at her first."[50] The Master Christ did not break the Law here; He said to them, yes stone her, but he who is without sin among you, let him throw a stone at her first. They began to leave one by one because they began to consider the situation in a different way. While they used to see themselves as righteous, and she, a sinful woman, their view was changed; she is a sinful woman and they are sinners also. Therefore, they went out one by one.

Then the Master Christ said to the woman, "'Woman, where are those accusers of yours? Has no one condemned you?' She said, 'No one, Lord.' And Jesus said to her, 'Neither do I condemn you; go and sin no more.'"[51]

The first point, thus, in anger management, is that you have to bear the responsibility for your anger, because you are responsible for *your* interpretation of

49 John 8:5.

50 John 8:7.

51 John 8:10–11.

the other's behavior. If you interpret their behavior in a sound way, you will be able to control your anger.

Slowness to anger

St. James says, "So then, my beloved brethren, let every man be swift to hear, slow to speak, slow to wrath."[52] I would like to focus here on the phrase "slow to wrath."[53] How do I slow down my anger, and bridle it and control it?

Imagine that you are driving a car, and this car has no brakes. This car will undoubtedly be an instrument of causing harm to others, and the occurrence of many accidents. To avoid the occurrence of an accident, two things must be available in the car: it must have good brakes, and you, as a driver, must be observing and steering accurately. This is because if there were an imminent danger before you, and you waited until the last moment before stopping the car, then you would hit whatever is before you even though the brakes were perfectly sound. Therefore, you have to observe the road

52 James 1:19.

53 This word, in the verse in Arabic, can be translated to "anger" but the NKJV translation used here uses the word "wrath."

well, and when you see danger ahead, you use the brakes at the right time, thereby avoiding a collision.

So also is the case with anger. You have to have good observation, and know when speaking with the other may be transformed into contention, where you become agitated, lose your temper, insult them, degrade them, and potentially hit them. Therefore, the person who has strong observation skills is able to stop their anger when they feels that they are about to clash with another. "My son, be wise, and make my heart glad, that I may answer him who reproaches me. A prudent man foresees evil and hides himself; the simple pass on and are punished."[54]

There are many things that can make a person slow to anger, and each of us ought to discover the brakes which may be used and by which we may attain benefit and profit. One person may make the sign of the cross and say, "Lord Jesus, help me." Another person may bring to mind the sufferings of the Master Christ on the cross, how He did not hide His face from the shame of spitting, and how He left His cheeks open to those who smite.[55] A third person may recite the "Our Father" prayer, so that it calms him down. A fourth person may

54 Proverbs 27:11–12.

55 The Divine Liturgy According to St. Gregory—*Agios* (Holy)

ask for the intercessions of one of the saints, so that they grant him calmness and peace. You have to discover the type of brakes which quiets down and slows your anger.

However, brakes alone are insufficient. You must have accuracy in steering and observation, and you need to realize when a collision can occur. If you feel great distress within and anger seeps into you, then do not wait until anger reaches its apex before you sign yourself with the sign of the cross, because, then, it will be too late to control your anger. There has to be good timing in addition to the brakes, so that you may be able to control your anger.

This matter requires a person to train oneself that they may be able to slow down their anger (as our teacher James the Apostle said).

"If you found in your houses scorpions
and snakes, would you not be diligent
in driving them out, that you may
live in safety in your houses?

And yet, here you are angry, and here
anger is taking root in your hearts, and
it cultivates in it rancor, and abundant
wood, and scorpions, and snakes."

— St. Athanasius —

The causes of anger

Know the cause of anger in your life. We said previously that the cause of anger is within a person and not without, so we cannot cast the responsibility on another person. The causes of anger, therefore, differ from one person to another; and consequently the methods of its treatment differ also.

1. The cause of anger for a person may be their lack of flexibility. They set their mind that a matter must be done in a particular way, and if something happens at variance with their way or their thought or their view, they become distressed and agitated and angry. For that person to come out victorious over their anger, they have to learn how to be flexible.

   We read in the Paradise of the Monks: "Be not a cube, but be a sphere."[56] This is because the cube does not move once placed in a location, but the sphere may be moved in any direction. The rounded person is able to deal with

56 A similar saying is attributed to Abba Muthues: "Now, he who sits among the brethren must not possess four corners, but he must be altogether round, so that he may move smoothly in respect of every man." *Paradise of the Holy Fathers* 2, W. Budge, trans. (Putty, Australia: St. Shenouda Monastery, 2008), 277.

others, and moves in all direction, and meets halfway[57] with others without sacrificing the truth. The cubic person, however, cannot move or adapt to others, nor can they meet halfway.

This we encounter often in marital problems. The husband and the wife have no flexibility, so this person cannot adapt to the other. The remedy lies within: how can we be more flexible with the other.

2. Of the causes of anger also is the lack of patience. For example, a person puts the key in the door but the key does not open the door for some reason. He gets angry, because he is impatient. Therefore, the Master Christ said, "By your patience possess your souls."[58] And in the parable of the sower, according to the Gospel of our teacher St. Luke, He says at the end of the parable when speaking about the good ground: "Bear fruit with patience."[59] I have to learn, therefore, how to be patient if I do not possess this virtue.

57 i.e. finding middle ground.

58 Luke 21:19

59 Luke 8:15

3. To another, the cause of anger is the ego,[60] and the ego shows in hypersensitivity.

   As one of the poets says, "... and touching silk makes his fingers bleed." That is, any word upsets and hurts him, and anything injures his dignity. He is a very sensitive person, and needs to be humbled a little to get rid of his hypersensitivity.

4. Another cause of anger also is the desire to control and have dominion. The controlling person is able to control others by one of two ways, and they can never be used together.

   The first way is violent anger. If I become agitated and scream with a loud voice, then people will fear me and give in to whatever I want to do, so that they may evade my rage. In this way, I have achieved my goal, which is controlling others and spreading terror in their hearts.

   As to the second way, it is deception and the employment of wile, so that I may make others perform my wishes and obey me.

60 Also: the self

I remember counseling a married man. His wife had a very controlling and dominating personality, and was very irascible. Because of this irascibility, her husband would evade the loss of her temper. As soon as she became irritated and lost her temper, the husband would say to her that he would do whatever she wanted. However, he was inwardly distressed, and felt that he always did all that she wanted, and could not do what he considered suitable.

A few years later, he also began to lose his temper and become irritated. When I met them, he began complaining that his wife was always irascible, and as a result of her irascibility, she did him wrong. The wife said, "You are the one who does me wrong and becomes irritated." I began following this heated dialogue between them, and I discovered that the wife had a dominating personality, and that he used to suppress his distress within until he lost control and began getting irritated and losing his temper.

I said to them in the end, "Both of you become agitated and lose your temper. But the loss of temper and agitation of the wife differs from the husband's. You are both similar on the outside." Therefore, when we give counsel, we have to know the causes of anger, and only then, can we offer the right remedy. They had the same manifestations on the outside, but their treatment is different. She becomes agitated and loses her temper because she wants to have dominance over others and to control them; he loses his temper because he kept having to accept humiliation and suppress it within, without expressing his distress. This is why he began to be agitated after many years.

I said to the wife that her treatment is to humble herself and put aside her wishes to have control and dominance, and to accept that the other may have a different opinion. I said to the husband that he must know how to express his anger and his distress, so that it is not transformed into suppressed feelings and bitterness, thereby suffering from diseases.

The expression of anger is very important. I have to mention that a particular behavior distresses me, but on the condition that I express my anger in a sound manner, without sin. This is what the Holy Scripture says, "Be angry, and do not sin."[61] We have to express our anger. In the Gospel of St. John, we read that one of the servants struck the Master Christ with the palm of his hand, so the Master Christ said to him, "If I have spoken evil, bear witness of the evil; but if well, why do you strike Me?"[62]

61 Ephesians 4:26.

62 John 18:23.

The Master Christ expressed His anger without falling into sin.

It is very important that you know the cause of anger which is within you, or within the person you are giving counsel to, so that you may help him get rid of this cause, whether it be inflexibility, or impatience, or hypersensitivity, or weakness in personality that he cannot express his opinion, or the desire to dominate and control others.

> "Beware that you may be sitting and thinking of judging your brother. For this uproots all the works of virtue, even though you had risen to the degree of perfection."
>
> — Saint Mar Isaac the Syrian —

Be transformed

To manage anger, it is important to think in a different way, for anger will not solve the problem, but it might make you unreasonable in your thoughts and actions.

Do not take decisions when you are edgy. Think in a reasonable and realistic way.

We have previously said that anger is a reaction to your interpretation of matters. So how can I interpret the matter in a different way? This is what is called "renewing of the mind." Paul the Apostle said, "Be transformed by the renewing of your mind."[63]

There might be a person who looks irascible, and it is said, "So and so is irascible; he looks jittery like this all the time." So how are we to be transformed? The answer is that I need to be renewed in my mind. That is, to think in a different way, and to look at matters in a different perspective.

For example, if I were sitting with a group of people in a hall, and I asked them to describe the hall, we would find that each of them would describe the hall in a different way, even though they are all describing the same hall. The reason for this difference is that each one sees the hall in a particular way. One might see the positives and speak of its vastness and lighting. Another person might see the negative things, because his gaze always falls on the negatives; he is always wrathful and angry, and there is nothing that he approves of.

63 Romans 12:2.

We need to renew our minds so that we may be able to look at things in a realistic and positive perspective. The realistic perspective does not mean that we say that evil is good, or good is evil, but it means that I possess a positive view, the way the Master Christ was in dealing with sinners. He never denied that they were sinners, but he looked at them in a positive way. He saw in them luminous things that were able to change their lives, like what happened with Zacchaeus the tax collector. People looked at him as a tax collector, as a sinner, as unjust and as a lover of money. But the Master Christ saw in him a person seeking God and looking for Him; therefore, He invited Himself to his house, and He said to him, "For today I must stay at your house,"[64] and also said to him, "He also is a son of Abraham."[65]

The word "renewing of the mind" means repentance, and repentance in Greek is *metanoia.*[66] When we hear the word *metanoia*, prostration instantly comes to mind, but its true meaning is repentance. The word *metanoia* consists of two words, "meta" which means "change" and "noia" which comes from the word *nous* which means "the intellect" or "mind" in Greek. So the word *metanoia*

64 Luke 19:5.

65 Luke 19:9.

66 This word is used in Arabic to mean "prostration."

means the change of the mind or the renewing of the thought.

When a person possesses the mind of Christ—"but we have the mind of Christ"[67]—he can see matters in a different perspective which will help him bear anger. Therefore, we have to train ourselves to see matters in a good way.

When a married couple comes to me, and the husband starts recounting many things about his wife, I ask him, "What are the good things she has done for you?" Believe me, I often find that it is difficult for him to remember the good things that she has done for him, and there are some who would even say to me, "She has done nothing good at all." I would answer him that this is not believable, for it is impossible that there is a person who has never done any good work in his life. I would then give him an exercise to note the good things his wife does, and to write them down in a notebook, so that we may discuss them together the next time.

The goal of this exercise is to try to change the person's perspective, so that he may see the positives, rather than the negatives only. When he sees the good things that are in the other person, then the intensity of the existing anger that is in him will diminish.

67 1 Corinthians 2:16.

The opposite of this takes place during the period of engagement, the period full of excessive sentiments. A person may not be able to see the flaws that are in the other person. We may advise one of them that this marriage will not continue, and that the other person is not suitable, but they are not able to discover their flaws because of the emotional perspective.

If they insist to get married, this perspective will be different after two or three years. All the good things which the husband used to see in his wife before marriage, he sees no longer now, because the perspective became different.

A person has to have a realistic, positive perspective, because this is very important in dealing with others.

Deal with the problem

We have to learn how to deal with problems, instead of getting angry and losing our temper, especially [when dealing] with problems that are called "irresolvable problems." There are many people who lose their nerves when faced with problems that have no solution. We have to learn how to deal with these kinds of problems.

An example of problems that have no solution are health problems. A person who has a disability; we can find that the person may deal with it in a sound way, calm from within, and not angry nor agitated; but another person may not accept his disability, and because of this disability, he is full of rage and hatred towards all those around him.

I remember, in this context, the story of Helen Keller who suffered from many disabilities. She was blind, mute, and deaf, and there was no solution for her problem, for she could not see, nor speak, nor hear. This may have made her a very irascible person, and spiteful. What sin did she commit that would make her suffer like that?

But Helen Keller dealt with the problem calmly and did not become angry. Firstly, she accepted her situation, that is, accepted the problem. There are many people who do not accept their situation, and the refusal to accept makes them irascible. Secondly, she dealt with her problem, adapted to it, and was able to speak, which is often an impossible thing for those who cannot hear.

We have in us a great energy. God has created us in His image and according to His likeness. This energy can make a person shatter the impossible. However, we do not use this energy for good, nor for the common interest, nor to improve ourselves, but we instead get angry and agitated, and we become indignant at society and at our situation.

Helen Keller lived over eighty years, and all those who contributed to the writing of her biography mentioned that she was a very peaceable person, full of inner peace and joy. The reason for this is that she did not reject her problem, but faced it and dealt with it. This is what we should do with situations which make us distressed and irascible.

I have to face the problem, and think about finding substitutes and solutions for it. Only then can I deal with it by the power of the Spirit of God who dwells in me. Anger will not solve the problem but will actually complicate the problem.

For example, when a married couple discusses the household budget and the husband feels that his wife is wasteful, as soon as they begin to plan to balance their expenditure and their income, he begins to be angry and agitated and insults her, humiliates her and sins against her. Here the one problem becomes two: the first problem is the budget, which remains unresolved, and the second problem is the humiliation that took place and the reciprocal insults between them. If the husband had dealt with the problem without losing his temper and without humiliating his wife, they would have had a single problem only.

I would like to reiterate: anger does not solve problems, but on the contrary it complicates the matter and multiplies the problems.

Expressing anger

Many of us do not know how to deal with negative feelings, nor how to communicate in a sound way, to express our anger. When there are negative feelings within us, we express them in one of three ways:

- We explode
- We suppress the feelings within us
- We express our inner feelings and negative feelings without sinning. This is the way we must follow, as the Holy Scripture said in Ephesians, "Be angry, and do not sin."[68] You have a right to express your anger, but you have no right to express it in a wrong way, but rather in a sound way. Expressing your feelings means having the ability to explain your feelings clearly and respectfully. How can I express my negative feelings in a sound way?

68 Ephesians 4:26.

"Do not think that anger is something to be taken lightly. The Prophet says, My eye is troubled by anger.[69] For the one whose eyes are ailing certainly cannot see the sun, and if he tries to look at it, it will harm him. So if you become angry, do not sin. Be angry and do not sin. For you, as men, become angry, whenever anger overcomes you, but you ought to sin not by keeping it in your hearts, because if you leave it in your hearts, anger turns against you, so it deprives you of seeing the light. Therefore, forgive others."

— St. Augustine —

You ought to express your feelings without speaking about your analysis of the other person's personality, because by doing so you judge them. No one can examine another person; God alone is He who examines the mind and heart.[70] Someone might say to you, "I feel that you do not trust me." This is neither a sensation nor a feeling. A sensation means that I am happy or I am distressed, etc. But "I feel that you do not trust me" is an analysis of the other person. If these words

69 Psalm 6:8 (Septuagint, Orthodox Study Bible).

70 Cf. Revelation 2:23 and Psalms 7:9.

were untrue, the other person may feel distressed, and the disagreement may be escalated between them. The proper expression is to say to him, "I feel hurt from what you have done." Here you are speaking about a behavior which could be measured and could be judged, but you cannot judge what lies behind this behavior.

As we have previously mentioned, when the Master Christ was struck by the chief priest's servant, He said to him, "Why do you strike Me?"[71] He did not analyze his personality, though the servant was related to Malchus whose ear Peter cut off. The Master Christ could have said to him, "Are you striking me to take vengeance for your relative whose ear Peter cut off?" or, "Do you strike me to please the chief priest?" If the Master Christ had directed to him these questions, He would have been judging him and analyzing his personality, though He has the right to do this, because He is the Judge of the whole earth, and He is the One who "searches the minds and hearts."[72] But the Master Christ said to him, "If I have spoken evil, bear witness of the evil; but if well, why do you strike Me?"[73]

When one of our children expresses their anger, we, as fathers and mothers, often reproach them, and we say

71 John 18:23.

72 Revelation 2:23.

73 John 18:23.

to them, "This is wrong; do not do this." We raise our children from infancy on not expressing their anger in a proper way. They, then, suppress their feelings inwardly until they grow up. The son, when he is all grown up, may either turn out rebellious, or may reflect all that was suppressed from infancy onto his parents, or his personality may be weak because he has not learned how to express his negative feelings in a proper non-sinful way.

Meditate on these sayings of St. Abba Poemen on the cure for anger:

- "If a man put the blame onto himself, to him, his brother would be more honorable than he, and better than he; and if he thought in himself that he was good, then, to him, his brother would be vile and shameful."
- "If you desire to find rest here and hereafter, say to yourself in every matter, 'I, who am I?' and judge no one."
- "Do not judge anyone, and do not slander any man, and God will grant you quietude and rest in the cell."

Therefore, we need to train ourselves on how to express our anger, wounds and feelings, without mistakes nor sin.

Pacification

What we mean by pacification is the attempt to control the outer motions[74] and the inner emotions.[75] The attempt to control does not mean that we deny these emotions, nor do we ignore or suppress them. This method is especially successful when dealing with those who think unreasonably and unrealistically. So if you were dealing with someone like this, it is to no avail that you say to him, "If I have spoken evil, bear witness of the evil; but if well, why do you strike Me?"[76] He will not accept these words. Therefore, I have to learn how to calm down my emotions. It is true that I neither ignore my emotions nor deny them, but I deal with them in the right way.

Of the things that help in pacification is changing the location. For example, when a married couple converses together, and their voices become raised and

74 Also: stirrings.

75 Or: feelings.

76 John 18:23.

they begin to be angry at each other, and yet in spite of this they insist on continuing the discussion, though in this way they will not reach a solution. Therefore, it is preferable that the discussion be postponed, and that they stay away from each other until they have both calmed down. Afterwards, they may think in a reasonable way in pursuit of solving the problem, and they may find alternative solutions, and put in place a realistic plan with God's help and the guidance of the Holy Spirit.

When you find that things have gone out of the scope of what is proper and fit, you have to calm down, and step away from that place, and replace the whole condition. Persisting in arguing when you have lost your nerves is an atrocious mistake.

Most of the wrong decisions are those which are made when you are nervous or angry. I advise you, therefore, to not make decisions when you are in such a state. You have to calm down first; then you will think in the right way.

The new man

Do you remember what God said to Cain? "Sin lies at the door. And its desire is for you, but you should rule over it."[77] That is, sin desires you, but you should rule over it. If these words were true for Cain, then for us they are most utterly true. We are a new creation in Christ Jesus;[78] we have put on, in Baptism, the new man.[79] Paul the Apostle, therefore says, "But now you yourselves are to put off all these: anger, wrath, malice, blasphemy, filthy language out of your mouth. Do not lie to one another, since you have put off the old man with his deeds."[80]

Of the traits of the old man who has died in Baptism are: anger, wrath, malice, blasphemy, filthy language. But the Apostle Paul says, "you yourselves are to put off all these, because we have put off the old man with his deeds," and we have put on, in Baptism, the new man, which is the creation of God. We have, then, the ability to deal with anger, by the power of the Holy Spirit who dwells in us.

"But the fruit of the Spirit is love, joy, peace, longsuffering, kindness, goodness, faithfulness, gentleness, self-control. Against such there is no law.

77 Genesis 4:7.

78 Cf. 2 Corinthians 5:17.

79 Cf. Ephesians 4:24.

80 Colossians 3:8–9.

And those who are Christ's have crucified the flesh with its passions and desires."[81]

God says to you that you are able to rule over sin, and to control your anger, and that you are able to change your temperament. God will give you this power that you may be victorious.

The Apostle Paul, therefore, presents to us three virtues. If we complete them in our lives, they will help us in managing anger, controlling it and ruling over it. He says, "Let all bitterness, wrath, anger, clamor, and evil speaking be put away from you, with all malice. And be kind to one another, tenderhearted, forgiving one another, even as God in Christ forgave you."[82]

These advices are:

- Be kind to one another
- Tenderhearted
- Forgiving one another, even as God, in Christ, forgave you

It is difficult for the kind person to lose his nerves and to become agitated quickly. The tenderhearted person is full of tenderness and compassion. The word tenderhearted means a heart that feels the pains of

81 Galatians 5:22–24.

82 Ephesians 4:31–32.

others. What distresses others causes me pain and hurts me and makes me suffer; and so I have tenderness in my heart. It is difficult for the tenderhearted person to hurt another person, because if he hurt someone, he, himself, would suffer inwardly. The tenderhearted person cannot direct hurtful words at another.

As for the forgiving person, he forgives the other his offenses, and forgets them, because a large portion of our anger is caused by a non-forgiving heart.

The bodily, psychological, and spiritual rest

Take care of your bodily rest. The man who is always going through distress after distress is like an inflated balloon, which as soon as you put pressure on it, it explodes. Therefore, it is very important that you take care of yourself, setting time for bodily, psychological, and spiritual rest, so that you relax.

There are some religious and spiritual people who feel that resting is sin, though the Master Christ in the Gospel of St. Mark said to His disciples, "Come aside by yourselves to a deserted place and rest a while."[83] St. Mark remarks: "And they did not even have time to

83 Mark 6:31.

eat."[84] It is as if the Master Christ wanted to say to His disciples, "We cannot finish the day this way. Therefore, we have to go to a deserted place away from people, so we may eat." The Lord Jesus who said to the devil, "Man shall not live by bread alone,"[85] is He who also said to His disciples, "Come to a deserted place that we may eat." This is because the Master Christ knows that the body is a talent,[86] and therefore, I must take care of the health of my body in a sound way.

There is a difference between giving comfort to the body, spoiling it, and caring for it for the glory of God. A man may lose his health and become weak, and as a result, he will not be able to serve God. Therefore, you have to care about your bodily health, eat nutritious food, get enough sleep, and exercise, to dissipate the nervous stress you have, and get rest. Comfort, laughter, a sweet smile, and friendly gatherings—these must occupy a place in your life. We have to learn from our beloved father, His Holiness Pope Shenouda, who with his customary smile and his gentle serene laugh, takes away from us many of the distresses we face.

You have to care about your spiritual health. You have to have spiritual friends with whom you converse,

84 Ibid.

85 Matthew 4:4.

86 i.e., a gift one is entrusted with (cf. Matthew 25:14–30).

and to whom you may vent in a safe atmosphere the stresses which you face. These spiritual friendships may be with the saints or with spiritual people you know. Likewise, your relationship with your father of confession and your spiritual guide is very important.

In counseling sessions, we work on preparing a safe atmosphere wherein a person is capable of revealing the stresses present in him, so that he may find rest. Only then can he deal with life wisely and without anger.

A specialist in counseling

In anger management, you may need to meet a specialist. It may be a psychiatrist or a doctor who specializes in giving counseling.

I would like to emphasize an important point, which is, not everyone who goes to see a psychiatrist [or therepist] is considered insane. Just as the body grows tired and gets sick and needs treatment, so does the mind[87] which may get tired and be in need of treatment. In the Book of the Wisdom of Sirach, it says, "Despise not the physician, for the Lord created him, and He grants healing by his hands."[88]

87 Or: psyche.

88 Translated from Arabic text. Cf. Wisdom of Sirach 38:1.

Anger might be because of what is called in psychiatry, "personality disorders," the matters that are disordered in the personality because of the conditions in which a person is raised or brought up. In this case, the person is in need of a specialist who could help him deal with the issue of anger.

Finally, I would like to remind you of the words of St. James: "For the wrath of man does not produce the righteousness of God";[89] and the words of St. Paul: "Be angry, and do not sin."[90] For anger is an energy which God has put in man so that he may use it for building up and not destruction. Therefore, we all need to know how to manage anger for the glory of the name of God.

Glory be to our God forever. Amen.

89 James 1:20.

90 Ephesians 4:26.

www.ingramcontent.com/pod-product-compliance
Lightning Source LLC
LaVergne TN
LVHW050944080826
845145LV00004B/1406
9781939972729